Health Treatment of Truth

The Unity of Life

AND THE

METHODS OF ARRIVING AT TRUTH

∞∞∞∞∞∞∞∞∞∞∞∞∞

∞BY∞

A* DISCOURSE,

MRS. MALINDA E. CRAMER,

At The Dedication of The

Home College of Spiritual Science

324 Seventeenth Street, San Francisco, Cal,

March 21st, 1888

INTRODUCTION

Rev. Natalie R. Jean

In search for Truth, I stumbled upon some articles and a book by Malinda Cramer. I later found out that these items were extremely rare. Most of Malinda Cramer's teachings perished in a fire in 1906. After reading her teachings, I find that there is a strong connection between Malinda Cramer and Emma Curtis Hopkins. I feel as though they were "Spiritual Sisters." With each passage, you feel as though you are receiving a healing. As I continue to bring Truth to the world, I felt that it was time to reintroduce these teachings to the world, so that Malinda Cramer's teachings can continue to thrive.

Be ready to speak have a greater understanding of your Being and to speak your Truth.

Home ○ College ○ of ○ Spiritual ○ Science,

324 Seventeenth Street, San Francisco, Cal.

Incorporated for Religious, Educational and Ethical purposes; for instruction in Spiritual Science and its therapeutic application.

One course of instruction consists of twelve lessons. Pupils received for one course, or for as many as may be necessary to fit them to become competent Teachers and Healers.

Classes, Tuesdays and Fridays, at 2 and 8 p.m.

Patients treated upon application, from 10 A.M. to 2 P.M. daily; except Sundays.

Students and Patients from the country can obtain rooms and board near the College.

All are benefited, and many restored to health and harmony of mind during the course of instruction.

Students from the College are in successful practice.

For terms of instruction and treatment, apply at the College, or address   M.E. CRAMER, PRESIDENT.

THE UNIVERSAL REGISTER.

Whatever any persons believe, they believe because they think it true. No one is prejudiced against Truth. All want the Truth, whatever it is, and wherever found.

The Universal Register is a book to contain names and addresses of those who thus want to know. All whose names appear on the Register become members of the Committee of Management; so, all being equally interested, should make an effort to obtain other names. Registers may be established in any centre throughout the world; and the names on each Register are forwarded from time to time to the Headquarters of the Great Register, which contains all names. Whenever a Centre is formed, the Members of the

Committee may call meetings for investigating Truth. The names and addresses on the Great Register will be printed from time to time, and copies forwarded to every centre. The Register thus becomes a Directory of Truthseekers. Centres are already established in many parts of the world.

OBJECTS.

That by union of thought, and united meditation and action, we may grow in Truth, outgrowing limitations; and by holding others in Truth, help them to overcome their limitations. A short time every Wednesday evening is devoted to meditation; also on the 27th of every month; all are requested to set apart a short time accordingly.

Many other advantages, which cannot be stated in short advertisement, will suggest themselves to readers. Add to your Faith, Works.

F.E. COOTE

2114 Mission Street, San Francisco, California, U.S.A.

Entered according to act of Congress, in the year 1888, by

MRS. M.E. CRAMER

In the office of the Library of Congress, at Washington.

THE UNITY OF LIFE,

AND THE

METHODS ◊ OF ◊ ARRIVING ◊ AT ◊ TRUTH.

The oneness of life or spirit is apparent in all things. We perceive the power of Divine Will at work in all nature, expressing itself in what may be called true prayer or aspiration. And that true prayer or aspiration is always the result of inherent Divine Will pressing us onward and upward-evolving a higher and broader consciousness-bringing us nearer in understanding to Spirit, the source of all being, and bestower of all blessings.

We perceive that all things in nature manifest a measure of conscious power, and are aspiring and working toward their source, ever asking and seeking by thought, word, or act, to come consciously "Nearer, my God, to Thee." The necessary means for further unfoldment is ever received or found. We recognize the power of Divine Love and Will at work in the seed, causing it to swell or expand (which is unfoldment), and burst the ground apart and come up to face the sunlight; and also in the vine, causing it to creep and find its way through unobserved crevices, in unthought-of ways, to reach the light and receive that which is necessary for its unfoldment and growth. So, even the plants teach us a lesson of true faith accompanied with works; which may be termed the prayer of acknowledgment or recognition; for they ask in action by acknowledgment of the source from which they draw, by the effort they make to reach the light and face the Sun.

The silent and inner word, which lies back of mental growth and action, aspiration and prayer, is the

THE UNITY OF LIFE

Divine Word, the Logos, which is to-day, yesterday and forever the same; and which is manifested or made apparent by the action of Divine Will through the Law of Justice. It works through the Soul in all degrees of expression, pressing on and on to a higher and broader consciousness, ever pointing toward the reality of its own being. Thus the process of evolution or Soul manifestation- is conducted. And all Soul unfoldment or manifestation may be said to be the result of Divine Will expressed in true aspiration, which moves alike in the seed, the plant, the animal, and man. So the real purpose of the Soul's endless variety of manifestations along the entire line of evolution is to image forth its possibilities, to project them in form, that it may look upon them and come to know itself and what true being or Spirit is.

It is impossible to perceive innate principles, or realize our divine nature, except through manifestation; for to perceive, three facts are necessary-the perceiver, the perception, and the thing perceived; and thus the human Soul declares her power, or demonstrates the divine principle of life, and proves her immortality, and that the spirit within is her light and life, and that the two are one. That is, through self experience we come to know the truth, and acknowledge "no other God before Me"- the One Infinite Spirit; for them we know that individual life and will is included within the Divine and Universal. Then the Outer becomes as the Inner, and His "Will is done on earth as it is in Heaven"; and we realize the kingdom within, which is the Spirit of God, who dwelleth in His Holy Temple. When we thus recognize His presence, and acknowledge the perfect good, and realize that our divine and eternal nature is His Life within, we have found the

THE UNITY OF LIFE

truth are freed; for the law is fulfilled, and the individual will has become universal, and the seeming struggles of life are finished.

What we most need to know in our present degree of unfoldment is, where and what Truth is; where and what Good is; or, where and what Spirit is; and of our relations to them, and of the relations of each to all, and of all to each. These are basic principles in Spiritual Science, and without them we cannot correct our errors of thought, and guide our minds to blend and unwaveringly harmonize with our inner light, which alone quickeneth and giveth us truth and wisdom. Until these most important truths and principles are clearly understood, the light shines in darkness, but the darkness comprehendeth it not- for God dwelleth at all times in all places, irrespective of our opinions, misinterpretations, and actions.

If we desire to possess the truth that is to make us free, it makes a very great difference in our work, or expression, whether we do or do not interpret truthfully and hold ourselves in truthful thought in relation to Spirit. We cannot change the eternal truth of God's omnipresence, or break His Law; but if, through ignorance or perversity, knowingly or otherwise, we act in opposition to the Law of Divine Will and Justice, which is also the law and will of our being, the Mind, acting in opposition to its source, will feel the inharmony of its own making at once in self-condemnation, dissatisfaction, or general harmony and confusion of thought. The worst that can result from false belief, or misinterpretation-the ultimate of its discord or inharmony-is the destruction of itself and its productions, or temporal forms of expression; but the Soul and Spirit it does not touch; they are truth and eternal; and Truth is Peace, Harmony, and Power. So, as long as we believe in

THE UNITY LIFE

evil and inharmony, and interpret ourselves and others relative to it, as being in and of it, we are showing disregard, or injustice, as it were, toward the perfect good in which we live and move and have our being. We want to awaken in understanding to that which is-to a realization of Omnipresent good and harmony, and to recognize its presence everywhere. We want to expand the consciousness, and awaken to Divine or Universal Truth, until we cease to hold in mind a thought that is in opposition to the Divine Principle within-until we cease to hold beliefs that are antagonistic to the all-pervading good; for they only environ our perception in mists of illusion.

Where justice towards the good is disregarded, it chastiseth the belief or thought which disobeys its law. Where justice toward the good is preserved in thought, it will preserve. "There is nothing so opposite to, and inconsistent with, the most holy power of God as injustice." So, love guided by Universal Justice, above all things conduces to the safety and happiness of humanity, and to the highest spiritual unfoldment. When once we are winged with true aspiration, there is no rest until we find the inner light, which is the Comforter, the spirit of the perfect good, the God, within; then our thoughts are at one with Truth, and the law of justice is observed toward the good; and we no longer carry discord in the heart and mind.

The perfect Good-the Spirit which pervades all-can never become less than itself; so, our beliefs about it cannot change the truth to its eternal unchanging condition. All are striving toward this goal, whether they know it or not; and in time all will come to unite in thought with good; and will acknowledge perfect being everywhere; and recognize God as the life of all beings. We can take our own time to do

THE UNITY OF LIFE

this. We may go as far from home, from Spirit, in understanding, as we will or like; even until all things seem or appear evil, dark, or inharmonious to our mental vision, and no ray of light is apparent to us to break the mists of this delusion. But even the light of God's presence is with us; His presence is bright is in the darkness, but the darkness apprehendeth it not. Then, to recognize His presence, and claim the perfect Good before all else in our thoughts and actions, and to discipline our minds in Divine Truth, is what is meant in the Scriptures by "becoming reconciled to God," and is a work of faith. But we want to Know how to speak the Word that unveils perception and manifests Good.

It is written, "The Word is nigh thee, even in thy mouth and in thy heart; that is, the Word of Faith, the Word which we preach." So the light of Truth is ever present in the silent, invisible Spirit within and around us; and is ours in manifestation as soon as we recognize and claim it. As soon as we claim it, by adjusting our thoughts, will, and desires to harmonize with it in quality of goodness, we become conscious of our union with, and are reconciled to Good. Truth is silent, and does not show forth until spoken. It is invisible, and does not appear in form on the sense plane until perceived and spoken in thought. Then, we need to know how to speak the Word of Truth, and how to acknowledge the light, and return home to the Father-to a spiritual consciousness-and this we can do, for all the power of Good, all the attributes of being, are winged with aspiration; always eager and striving for the higher and true path which leads home to the Father, to a knowledge and realization of Being and Reality.

For the purpose of acquiring and imparting a knowledge of Spiritual Science, classes have been held in

THE UNITY OF LIFE

our home during several months past, which proved of great value to pupils and teachers. In consequence of which, my husband and I concluded to lay the foundation for a broader future work. Upon interior examination, we find that the inner light and life is pressing us on in the way in which we began; and we feel it a divine duty to go on seeking and giving the truth in the way that to us seemeth best. So willing are we to comply with this duty, both in the silent instruction of the treatment, and by oral lesson or spoken word, that we turn not from it, but are ready to go onward and ever on, seeking to come nearer and manifest more of the Life, that lighteth the Soul; without desire to look back and cling to things of the past; contended in the Eternal Now. In this work we find the way to blend our thoughts, desires, and will to act in conscious harmony with the Universal. For the purpose of continuing our work, we have organized and chartered. The Home College of Spiritual Science. We have not chosen this name because it is located at our external temporal home, which is but a most external and unreal symbol of the esoteric or spiritual meaning of the word. "As a thousand rays emanate from one flame," so do all souls of all external things emanate from the one Eternal Spirit which is God. And they are Temples of the Living God; for "in our Father's house there are many mansions"; and each soul of every external form is a temple of mansion which the Father, the Infinite Spirit, pervades. So, Infinite Spirit is our Home. It is the Home of the Soul; always was; and always will be. This does not pertain to locality, for Spirit "bright all space doth occupy," and is here with us at this time as much as any place in the Universe. And when our vision is opened to Truth, the attributes of Spirit, which are Divine Mind, become manifested by us, and we see with eyes and hear with ears that the worldly mind knows not of; and we know

THE UNITY OF LIFE

that we are enveloped, embraced within, and suffused by Divine Spirit, which is God.

This College is formed for religious, educational, and ethical purposes; for instruction in Spiritual Science, and its therapeutic application. Also for preparing pupils to become competent teachers and practitioners in the Science, and of issuing diplomas to graduates as a recognition of fitness. Also for organizing and establishing Schools or Colleges of Spiritual Science in any Territory or State in the United States. For the purpose of giving silent lessons or treatments to pupils who believe, in sickness, inharmony, and evil.

METHODS.-One course of instruction will consist of twelve lessons. The classes in Metaphysics will embrace Lessons upon Being or Reality, its manifestation and unfoldment; upon Thought, its relation to Spirit and Matter, or the inner and the outer, as the creative or revealing principle. Also a lesson upon the attributes or qualities of Mind, and how to adjust our thoughts in harmony with them, and become conscious of our unity with the Universal. Upon true prayer and faith, as being knowledge sought and gained. Upon Spiritual Perception and Intuition, and to how unfold them. Upon the power of the Divine Word, its symbol or sign. And upon the Spoken Word, and the purpose of life in creation.

These lessons are arranged in such a manner as to discipline mind, and enable the students to perceive and realize the truth for themselves. All the powers of Spirit are invisible and silent; and when spoken and made manifest, they are born of Spirit. "There is diversity of gifts by the same Spirit; to one is given the word of Wisdom; to another Word of Knowledge by the same Spirit; to another

THE UNITY LIFE

Faith; to another gifts of Healing." Then in Spirit consists all Power; and the true method of education must be the one that will educate the mind to reveal or unfold Spiritual power, or to recognize Truth.

We have adopted methods in teaching which will unfold the inner and divine nature, and enable the pupils to perceive the truth that will free them from the delusions that veil the understanding from the light of truth, and to rise in consciousness above the border-line of elemental thought to the Spiritual plane of Truth and Reality. This can only be done by the unfoldment of our own Divine Nature. The Kingdom of Heaven can be enjoyed here, now; for it is always with us; and all can enter it when they know and love the Truth, and acknowledge Spirit before all else. Many have travelled this path, and found the Realm of Wisdom and Harmony, "The Comforter"; and what one has found, all may. All methods of Teaching should aim to unfold the divine nature, and aid the pupil to this Realm. There is no religion higher than Truth; and Spiritual Science is truly a religious science. The term "religion" may be interpreted to mean: related to, bound back, or relationship with God; and a true religious or metaphysical system is based upon Spiritual Truth, and will define the true terms of that relation. The Truth embodied in all religions is Eternal, and is alive in the hearts of the people to-day; and the wave of Spirituality (the New Illumination that is quickening the hearts of the people at this time, and awakening them to perceive the unity of truth, which underlies all religions,) is Spirit recognizing its own Truth. "We can have no conception of God-wisdom but by knowing the order and manner in which acts." Spiritual Science leads to this knowledge; and it is by understanding His Science that we may perceive and come face to face with the perfect Good. "And when that which is perfect is

THE UNITY LIFE

come, that which is in part shall be done away"; the imperfect will drop from our mind. Another great Teacher has said, "He who would hasten toward the good must cease to see evil.: By Spiritual Science we shall be able to know the Good, and that it is everywhere. As Elias Hicks, the Quaker, has said: "God fills all things, and is everywhere present. The grace of God that bringeth salvation appeareth to all men. This must comprehend all mankind, who have a thousand different notions about outward exercises in religious matters, in which there is no religion at all."

There is no religion or science in anything but in Spirit, and in being taught by it and coming under its leading. There are many Schools and Colleges that are working in this direction. What we want are more Schools and Colleges, that will teach us how to recognize that which is and always was; or to perceive that Truth which never changes-Schools and Colleges where the methods of teaching will awaken us to a knowledge of our Immortal Selves, and reveal the good from within; thus enabling us to become conscious of the reality of the life "in which we live and move and have our being," and save ourselves the discords and delusions which arise from going counter to the law in thought.

Before we can reach any great degree of illumination and power we must know the Truth, and exalt Spirit in thought as it is in reality, by claiming it in thought, word, and act as master over matter; and thus bend and shape our thoughts to harmonize with this truth and the Attributes of Spirit. The Comforter spoke of in the Scripture is the Spirit of Truth, the light and life of God manifesting in the Soul. Jesus told his disciples that it would not go out of them, "for it dwelleth in you and shall be in

THE UNITY OF LIFE

you." We want to know how to realize these truths, and how to discipline our minds to harmonize with or express them; and that the Saviour is God manifesting Himself in Humanity; for no one knows the things of God but the Spirit of God. So when we, as Spiritual Scientists and Metaphysicians, take ourselves through a thorough course of mental training; that we may realize the things of Spirit, the now hidden truths and mysteries of life unveil themselves to us. "Now we see through a glass darkly, but then face to face." When once we awaken to Spiritual Consciousness, we grow in power for good by living the truth; by making our innermost thought and external act harmonize with Truth and Justice. No one becomes a Messiah by speculating upon Divine doctrines without practising them; for what we think we become in word and deed. To think truth is harmony and power; and this we cannot have by merely adopting creeds and beliefs. The Soul must demonstrate the Divine Principles by manifesting Her Immortal qualities, and this declare or prove Herself to be a child of God. This is a state of perfect Faith that can only come by Works.

The truths in all religious teachings are identical, so far as their universal element is concerned. The Spiritual and true ideal of all religion is the unfoldment of Self-the Soul's divinest qualities, and the harmonious development of all its powers to the highest degree. This Science is Universal Truth; and the essential spirit or truth of all ages, all nations, and all times belong to it. It teaches thorough self-respect, and free self-devotion to great and divine ideas. The proofs we have that this Science is thoroughly practical are the divine and noble efforts made, and self-sacrificing love shewn for the truth by our pupils when it is perceived by them. And in this love of Truth for its own sake lies the only hope of the spiritual awakening of the inner and divine

THE UNITY LIFE

man, and of the consciousness of the Unity of Life. This Science gives us Faith in humanity as belonging to the one Infinite Good; it points the way by which the individual may expand his consciousness an reason, and guide them higher and higher toward the Supreme Powers of his Being. So our work is to educate the pupils to realize the harmony of the Universal; to teach them that they are noble and divine, here and now; and cause them to realize the ever-present God, and how to grow more and more like Him.

This truly religious science proclaims the great brotherhood of mankind, without limit or bound; it awakens us to a knowledge of our relationship not only to one Church and Nation, but to all Churches and all Nations; not only to one Planet or System of Planets, but to our unity with Infinite life; and we are ready to acknowledge our oneness with all, and receive truth from everything, of every degree and station in the boundless Universe. As there is no place where God is not; there is no place-as Emerson says-that we are not akin to. And when in our divinest state of mind, we shall feel this union regardless of what the senses reveal. In this unity, which underlies all nature-in the Valley of Silence-we find God; as did Father Ryan, who says:

"Do you ask what I found in the Valley?
'Tis my trysting place with the Divine.
And I fell at the feet of the Holy;
And around me a voice said-Be mine.
Then rose from the depths of my Spirit.
An echo-My heart shall be thine."

THE UNITY LIFE

When we entered our home two years ago, it was silently dedicated to Truth, and the preparation for our present work has been in process of unfoldment from that time. The home thus consecrated is the principal place of business of the "The Home College of Spiritual Science." The term "Spiritual Science" means to us the science of life, or the method of Spirit in manifestation. There is no Truth that is not included in Spirit; and Science is co-eternal with Spirit. Them, to Truth, to the Good, we dedicate the Home College of Spiritual Science.

To Universal Spirit-in which we live and move, and have our being, which is our Eternal Home, the "House of many mansions"- we dedicate the Home College.

To the Source of all Truth, the bestower of all blessings, the life of all things, we dedicate this College.

Then, "as much truth as in me is, I am ready to teach the Gospel"; in other words-as much truth as we know we will teach. But we will ever ask and seek of the Spirit within, and as we receive we will give. To Truth, then, wherever found, and to this work, there comes from the depths of my soul an echo-"My hearth shall be Thine."

THE UNITY OF GOOD

BY MRS. M.E. CRAMER

"Where the Spirit of the Lord is, there is liberty."
"Receive ye one another, as Christ also received us to the glory of God."

There is probably no statement that Divine Scientists, as a body, love to make more frequently than the declaration that "all is good." This statement is broad, generous, and all-inclusive-one that stands the close inspection of divine perception and the true analysis of divine reasoning. However, not all attempts to analyze the nature of the declaration are based in unity; neither are they uniformly free from traditional belief of duality.

Since all true analysis is from Principle, the first and highest or the last and absolute analysis of all things is to be found in Principle-a Source "without variableness, or shadow of turning;" one ever the same and always to be relied upon as a basis for true reasoning. The first requirement for a true analysis of this subject is knowledge of what the All-Good is –what the true nature of it implies. Zealous and enthusiastic natures, when they first hear that the All-in-all is Good, are eager to find a place in the Good for former opinions and beliefs-for all feelings and circumstances, of whatever nature or type. They seek to portray their beliefs of how "all things" are found to be good and sourced in God. Their first attempt, perhaps, is an effort to realize the freedom of Truth and oneness with the All-Good by calling error of belief, contradictory statements, aches, pains, inharmony, and poverty good, and by claiming that so-called sin, sickness, and death are traceable to God, who is Good, is Health, and is Life. Such attempts at solving the problems of life do not prove freedom nor bring satisfaction, and there necessarily follows an opposite feeling of discouragement, out of which come theories of postponement and "hope deferred." These theories are not essentially different from the old

THE UNITY OF GOOD

doctrines of a "heaven after death" and "good for the future."

With the sudden joy that comes to such persons, at The dawn of the wonderful truth of the infinitude if Good, that "I and my Father are one" (I am one with all that is), there comes a feeling of great energy; they want to work, write, speak, and interpret. The Spirit of Power-Unity-is upon them, and act they must. But if such would work quietly, in a state of mental peace, they would temper their zeal and enthusiasm with the consciousness of divine judgment, the analysis of true reason, the discrimination of justice. They would be able clearly to define the law of unity and speak with authority. They world work with certainty and abide unwaveringly in the true meaning of the statement that "like produces like," that "what is begotten [or born] of Spirit is Spirit," that what is born of Spirit "sinneth not, its seed [the word] remaineth in it, and it cannot sin because it is born of God."

In this day of scientific research, when so many are seeing the wonderful truth of the unity if the whole (that there is but one Substance, Mind, or Spirit in the universe), is it not essential to the maintenance of this consciousness that we adjust our ways, by true analysis, to this –the greatest good ever known? Permanent realization is just consideration of nature and goodness of the Whole.

Christ's consciousness of unity with one omnipresent Spirit, or Mind, the All-Good, and that what is expressed of Spirit, or Mind, is the same substance, did not cause him to portray so-called sin, sickness, or death. He was consciously free from such appearances. Then, if his

THE UNITY OF GOOD

oneness with God made him free from such appearances, how could God, at any time, be the Source of them?

Friends, justice and freedom cannot be separated. Think you that the healing of the sick and raising of the dead, in either ancient or modern times, are accomplished through individual ability to do away with what is sourced in Omnipotence, Omniscience and Omnipresence-the one and only Being? Until we see that the unity of Good is the unity of God, that the word *God* stands for the All-Omnipotence. Omniscience, and Omnipresence-and that we in no way differ from it, either in spirit, soul, or body, we do not appreciate the true presentation of Divine Science.

This law of unity is power. Since power is incapable of division, the demonstrations of power are united or organized effort and methods of applying it. Every successful movement for the advancement of the cause of Truth, or for the successful carrying out of any enterprise, must be based in unity of power, unity of purpose of action. This law of expression is power manifesting itself through true motive and in perfection action. Cooperation of work, word, and deed is what our consciousness of the unity of good must actualize throughout the world. What is divinely perceived to be true must necessarily actualize-be made visible and spread abroad. There is no invisible truth that shall not come forth and be made visible.

As Universal Brotherhood is based in Universal Fatherhood, the successful actualization of any cause that is for the good of humanity must find its origin in the one Source in which we all have being, and be based in the never-ending unity of Good. Organized effort is a natural

THE UNITY OF GOOD

sign following the true consciousness of unity. There can be no division in purpose, since there is none in power.

We have, for years, earnestly and unwaveringly advocated organization and association based in consciousness of unity. It has been a pioneer work. We have met with many who have come out of churches and societies not thus consciously based, and who so feared the words "organization" and "association" that they would give the work no consideration whatever. We have met with some who so feared that they would come into bondage through indorsing united effort that they hampered their own endeavors and did not succeed. They were really making some past experience the basis for action; and their judgment as to what constitutes freedom was based therein.

In escaping from any supposed bondage it requires a fine discrimination to discern whether our conclusions are based in Principle or prejudice. If based in prejudice, like a pendulum they swing to the opposite extreme, but are not long fixed in one place; if based in Principle, they see the truth of association and of all things, and are not afraid.

We have also met with those who could readily see that organization is the law of the Universe-that nothing is accomplished without association. That it is based in Unity is everywhere manifest in the living works of God. Many have made this the basis for their work. Such are successful, and are practically united with us in spirit, in our endeavor to universalize the demonstration of the unity of Good. What is good and practical for individual success and demonstration is equally so for humanity as a whole. Thus we are encouraged to stand firm and to persevere in presenting our ideas of associated effort. Now that you in

THE UNITY OF GOOD

the East are endeavoring to unity the liberal workers the world over, we are one in purpose, and we say, "God speed your good work!" If our efforts are based aright our buildings will stand the test of eternity, and nothing can prevail against them.

The question is often asked, "Are the Divine Science centers, whose teaching is based in unity, independent of one another?" We hold that inasmuch as they are based in the unity of Mind, or Spirit, or the truth of God manifesting himself here and now in creation, they are at one; not dependent upon one another, nor yet independent, but a unit-an undivided whole: hence, concerted action must be the natural sign following. This is the "Spirit of the Lord," in which there is liberty.

So far as any work is based in unity, it is built on a rock foundation. This each center should try to convey. There are no divisions in truth; no opposite qualities nor attributes; no high nor low. Our various ways of expressing Truth do not stand for differences, any more than do the various demonstrations in the science of numbers: they rather testify if the infinity of Truth. Statements that contradict each other, though upon the same subject, are the only differences we have to minimize. Since but one of them can be true of the subject, the other has no power to oppose it.

We are co-workers with God, and our message of Truth to the world is the revelation of what Being is. This revelation is illumination and permanent help to all people. It is equally the privilege of each one to proclaim the Truth of Being, which is "glad tidings of great joy" to all people. Our true words of unity are as a great light shining equally upon all.

THE UNITY OF GOOD

To believe that a knowledge of good and evil is good to make wise is to believe that the Source of wisdom is a contradiction. If the Source and cause of wisdom, or any other good quality, were composed of opposites, we could never have any but contradictory experiences. But since the Source and Cause of all things are one, to think and believe aright is to have no contradictory experiences; it is to experience harmony and absolute good in our feelings and environments. Inasmuch as the Source of all living existence is One, one partakes of forbidden fruit when he proclaims a dual basis for wisdom or any other aspect of Being.

In Divine Science we hold that error has no claim upon spirit, soul, or body. We keep the three in state of at-one-ment and see man as God-expressed. The supposition that I have "a higher self and a lower self" places *me* nowhere. The I Am, which is supposed to be something subject to both, must fight and put down one and exalt the other to bring him to power. This I Am must occupy a very difficult position. Just who the one is that stands between the two, and exalts one of the detriment of the other, is not clearly defined in any of the dual theories. Friends, let us not deceive ourselves by accepting such theories for the truth of Unity. We Scientists cannot Afford to hold so uncertain and un-Godlike a position. We cannot conceive of God holding such relationship or spending His time battling with opposing natures; and it is self-evident that we cannot take an entirely different position and be His true followers.

To overcome any false claim, the first requisite is to know the truth that of which the claim is untenable. As soon as the claim is seen to be false, it is at an end; we are willing to drop it. There is nothing higher than Truth, and

THE UNITY OF GOOD

Truth is not too high to be practically demonstrated in all the walks of life. We cannot do a greater good than to teach people the highest –The Absolute, the living Principle of all things.

There are not two minds. It is to be understood that in Divine Science we do not admit that our bodily existence is separate and apart from Spirit, or Mind, which are synonymous. The word *Mind* is used, not in the sense of there being minds many, but as a name for the All-in-all. So powerful is the truth that what is begotten of Mind is Mind, or that the All-in-all is Mind, to make itself felt when held to, that the whole body is illumined with divine consciousness. This is so far above the commonly accepted statement-that Infinite Mind and Body are unlike in substance-that such a declaration seems almost a hallucination. We have demonstrated the Absolute Truth is the power that quickens anew and proves that the body is as free from inharmony as is Infinite Mind. We do not realize the possibilities inherent in its substance until we accept the unity of the whole as Eternal Truth, and make it a basis for our work. Also, we have proved that, in healing, the most necessary denial to make is: "There is no separation from God; there is no law apart from His own nature."

An incontestable point in Divine Science that is, because the one All is Good, a realization of this fact dispels the supposition that Man is dual in nature, or of dual power, And of dual actions and results in his life. It dispels the supposition of sin, innate or otherwise, and brings out the highest demonstration of health (wholeness). Many seemingly incurable cases have been healed by means of our consciousness of the unity of Good. If we entirely disown the supposition that there is a self other than the Son of the Most High, one who is God's own

THE UNITY OF GOOD

image and like Him in nature, we shall likewise destroy all sense of disease and sin. If we cease partaking of "good and evil" we cease believing that we are dual-mortal and immortal, human, and divine, temporal and eternal; in short, that we are contradictories. Thus we do destroy opposites in feeling and enjoy unity, harmony, and permanent health.

"No man can serve two masters;" neither can he serve two natures. The All-Good has been set forth, and each one can say "I am It;" this is the ultimate. This does away with all that duality claims. As "a tree is known by its fruit," we should have a higher conception of the qualities of our being than to suppose they are subject to evil (that they fall short of truth); we shall come to know that the following words have no meaning in true Being: Death, hate, error, corruption, ignorance, illusion, weakness, injustice, doubt, war, inharmony, and postponement. These words simply stand for would or might be, where God, the Good, not All-in-all. So they do not represent what really is.

Can we not all rejoice in the gospel of "glad tidings"-that there is no death nor dead matter in the whole universe, and no evil substance or power? As we know the unity of Good and exercise our knowledge in all our ways, we enjoy fruit that is in perfect accord with our knowledge; hence, its universal exercise by mankind would be universal supply, or plenty. In the practice of the unity of Good is contained all the good implies. The exercise of any one of the qualities of Being must have the same effect as the exercise of any other. The practice of justice, for example, has the same good result as does the practice of love, or of knowledge, wisdom, intelligence, power, truth, peace, or harmony. The All-Good is one and inseparable; so, if we

THE UNITY OF GOOD

offend in any one of these qualities we offend in the whole. The full practice of the good results in its full demonstration. As health, happiness, success, prosperity, and plenty belong to the good, they must necessarily be the demonstrated results of its practice.

Do we know the *truth* that we are *It*, or do we believe that it comes to us from afar? Are at one with God and still ignorant? Do we listen to a voice apart from ourselves, or has God's voice become ours? Think what unity means, what the Oneness of Life implies, what the Goodness of the Whole reveals! Shall we not perceive one another as Christ received us, to the glory of God-that God, the Good, may be known as All-in-all?

BASIC STATEMENTS

And

HEALTH TREATMENT OF TRUTH

A System of Instruction in

DIVINE SCIENCE and its
APPLICATION in HEALING

And for

Class Training, Home and Private Use

Perceived Through a Study of Divine Science and Proved Through Repeated Demonstrations to be Applicable Alike to All in The Demonstration of Health, Happiness, and Prosperity

---

NINTH EDITION REVISED

By
M.E. CRAMER

Author of "Divine Science and Healing"

Denver. Colorado
1917

PREFACE
§

The arrangement of this consecutive course condensed lessons, under the heading of BASIC STATEMENTS AND TREATMENTS, is designed to be a simple, practical method which, when understood and practiced, will enable students to realize wholeness for themselves, and others. Wholeness is comprised of pure Being, perfect thought and result. It is the all of Life, Love, Truth, Intelligence, Substance, Power, and Presence for which we are seeking. It means Health, Satisfaction and Success.

CONTENTS
§
PART I

BASIC STATEMENTS OF DIVINE SCIENCE FOR HEALTH TREATMENT

I. Healing by the Christ Method..................................34

BE SINCERE IN YOUR EFFORTS

PART II

Introductory..46
Directions for Application of Treatment..........................48

WHAT TO ACCEPT AND WHAT TO REJECT

I. Statement of Being. At-one-ment is Harmony. At-One-ment is Salvation. Agree with Thine Adversary Quickly. Treatment-Wholeness..........................51
II. Know the Truth and the Truth Shall Make You Free. Treatment- Perpetual Health Against Mortal Intelligence..................................55
III. I have Overcome, Treatment-Adjustment for The helping of Environment...................57
IV. Treatment – Ilumination. Dehypnotizes from Erroneous Beliefs of Subjection..............59
V. The Way of Life. Perfection of Body............60
VI. Straight is the Gate and Narrow the Way Which Leadeth unto Life. Treatment-Dominion Over All Suffering...................................62
VII. Treatment – Opulence..................................64
VIII. He that Believeth on Me, the Works That I Do Shall He Do Also. Treatment – Demonstrate The Comforter..65
IX. Like Expresses Like. Treatment against Bodily Limitation and for Demonstration of Opportunities 67
X. Specific Treatment for Dominion................69

XI. Specific Treatment against the Desire for Liquor 70
XII. Treatment-Truth for General Bodily Healing 71
XIII. Treatment – Perfect Sight...........................72
XIV. Treatment – Healing of All Acute Diseases.72
XV. Treatment – Perfect Digestion....................74
Brief Summary..75

PART ONE
§

DIVINE SCIENCE STATEMENTS

AND

HEALTH TREATMENT

DIVINE SCIENCE STATEMENTS

AND

HEALTH TREATMENT

§

HEALING BY THE CHRIST METHOD

The basis for the manifestation of power in the Christ Method of Healing us knowledge of at-one-ment of man and God. "I and my Father are one" means one and the same in nature, possibility, and power; not two Beings, Spirits or Minds. The Creator of an ever-present living creation must necessarily be infinite and limitless from eternity to eternity; hence, there can be neither finite being nor limitation.

Most people believe in creation to be an event of the past, and that creative action ceased with the accomplishment of that event. Where this is believed, it is claimed that creation belongs to time and place. This claim cannot be true, for all that live, live within and unto God, and are, therefore, living within the omnipresent Creator throughout eternity; and must be, begin, end and be complete in God *now*. If Being and the beginning of its expression were not eternal, existence would have no relationship with God at this time. "The way, the truth, and the life," must be the origin of all living things; hence, all things must in the end find their abiding place in Being where they have origin, which makes them eternal. As "I Am" is the Word which is the light of the world, and of every man that comes into the world, everything lives within Me and is illumined with My glory, even as the burning

CHRIST METHOD OF HEALING

bush was to Moses, aflame with the light of My Holy presence.

Not until we conceive that all things are now alive unto God's eternity and wholeness, and not unto time, shall we "witness the beginning of creation." When we cease thinking, speaking and acting, as if the body, or anything pertaining to it, belongs unto time, and is dependent on place, we shall have ceased talking about death and planning for the grave. A full understanding of Divine Science, the living truth of what we are, is a Knowledge of God in creation, that creation is God expressed.

HEALING

There are various ways by which the attention of people may be arrested and called to the Christ Method of Healing. Some are interested through hearing of the healing of others and are thus caused to give it consideration. Wanting healing, as they do, either for themselves or friends, they are induced to try this method, and as it results in the health and satisfaction for which they have long sought, they in turn are ready to interest others.

They who say, "if one can be healed, another can, hence, healing is for me," speak wisely. They virtually declare the vital truth for themselves-that "There is no respect of persons with God." This decision is good, it comprehends much, it is a receptive attitude which is ready for successful results. Again, others are advised by friends to try the Christ Method, and as they have done all they knew to do-having exhausted every method that has been presented for the salvation of man-they accept the advice,

DIVINE SCIENCE STATEMENTS

and resolve to try the Truth, which to know makes them free, and are made whole.

The ways by which people are led to investigate Divine Science and practice it may vary; but what all are seeking to know is, *when* and *how* to begin. *Now* is always the accepted time, the only time to begin. The moment you want to be healed is the right time to commence the work. It is understood by all that there can be no result without a cause, and cause can bring forth no result without a cause, and cause can bring forth no result without action so *now* is the time to act and produce results. No one can enjoy health as a result of treatment until the treatment is commenced. Hence, the beginning must necessarily precede the result. There is something for each one to do who wants healing, though the nature of the work to be done may differ from all previous attempts made to regain health. Much has been said in the class-room, written and published, explanatory of methods by which healing is done, which are considered helpful in their nature; but in the Christ Method, a knowledge of Being that which is whole, is the one thing necessary as a basic Principle for demonstration.

How can we heal others, see them whole, when there is a beam in our own eye? The supposition that there is something in our nature that it the opposite of God will see motes and blemishes in others; for that which sees and describes false belief as real, is itself false belief. Knowledge never believes error to be truth. When a child understands the principle by which to solve his problem, he neither believes that error is truth, nor that a mistake stands for calculation.

CHRIST METHOD OF HEALING

The responsibility as to the result of treatment does not rest exclusively with the person employed in giving treatment. Christ, in the patient, who is "The Way, the Truth, and the Life," compels no personified false beliefs to accept Him, and think and believe that they are whole. God creates all things, but does not create opinions concerning them. It is a matter of choice, called free will, whether we pronounce with God or otherwise. "Choose ye this day whom ye will serve," whether it be the Truth that the infinite whole is God, and is perfect, or whether it be the false supposition that there is something else, that is imperfect. Those wanting to be healed should do their part and be willing to recognize and receive unto themselves the Truth that they are whole. The record of Life, the truth of Being, says that we have eternal life with God. This being true, we must necessarily have eternal health in God, and be satisfied and happy.

The teaching of Jesus stands above all teachings preceding it, in that He taught that knowledge of the Truth applied, heals, or puts an end to sickness; for there can be no sickness in God or Good, hence can be none in Truth. His practice proved the truth of His preaching, for He not only healed the sick when called upon to do so, but His command to the disciples was to go forth into all the world, and preach the gospel unto every creature, and heal the sick. It is not sufficient to enable us to demonstrate wholeness that we think the truth for a portion of creation, for Truth must erase the false belief of the world's apostasy from God; and thus proceed forth with the Holy Spirit into all the world, even unto the ends of the earth.

"Go show yourselves to the Priests," Jesus said unto the ten lepers who called upon him to have mercy on them. The appeal was made as he approached, which,

DIVINE SCIENCE STATEMENTS

spiritually speaking, made the conjunction or at-one-ment in thought, between, them; they went their way, which was according to his direction or commandment; hence, the result was they realized that they were whole, and were clean.

The first requirement in this method of healing is that of giving up the false supposition and unsatisfying belief of a self-hood separate from God. This change of conception is the spiritual act of baptizing unto repentance, which precedes the taking on of at-one-ment-the baptism of the Holy Spirit. At-one-ment is the yoke that is easy,-the bond of union which makes every burden light.

Where two are agreed upon earth as touching any one thing there is at-one-ment, and *I am* is in the midst of them with perfect demonstration. What is agreed upon shall be granted unto them. No line is to be drawn between the one employed in giving treatment and the one receiving it. The two should agree, and thus be one receiving it. The two should agree, and thus be one in the Truth, of which they seek demonstration. If it be health, the freedom and harmony of Truth, that is sought to be realized, the first thing to do is agree that *health is*, and is for *you* and if for *you*, it is *present*; what is not present cannot be realized, enjoyed, or demonstrated. In this you have the whole plan of success. You have now determined to shape your thought, word, and deed, according to the Truth of what *is*; and is for *you*, and it at hand. So, there is no postponement, neither is there seeking for something to come from afar; what you ask for is come; is yours now.

"No" should never be taken for an answer, and in order to prove that "No" is not an accepted answer you are to cease making negative claims and doing that which is

CHRIST METHOD OF HEALING

contrary to Truth. God accepts no excuses, even as the principle in mathematics admits no excuses in the solution of a problem, but demands that the principle be adhered to if demonstrated in the example. Make your claims according to Truth. Claim to be Truth, and your words will be the words of Life-the pure white "Yes" of God. Let man, created in Christ Jesus, in righteousness and holiness of Truth, use the pronoun I as meaning the unlimited nature of the All Good. The Canaanitish woman was so determined to have her daughter healed that she refused to recognize any obstacle to that result. All should be thus determined who ask for healing, and the result following will be the same as it was with her.

As the word that is with God, and is God, made the world, and is it light and life, one should stop discussing the question as to whether it is God's will that we be whole,- made to enjoy health. The will of an all-powerful God make whole must of necessity be one and the same at all times. God must be without variation and the same at all times. God must be without variation or shadow of turning. His will must be for the absolute perfection and goodness of each one in every respect. The habit of setting up obstacles, claiming difficulties, and making excuses should be given up. The infinite All, when accepted as being all Good, God, proves to be health, success and harmony without limit. After having heard the Truth, nothing but a willingness to continue in old lines of belief and tradition can hinder any one from having a realization of wholeness. Since it is God's will that all should feel well, and right habit thought based in Being will bring this about, there is no reason why all should not enjoy health in the knowledge of Truth. It is an easy matter to reject the belief that there are difficulties to be overcome, obstacles in the way, excuses to be made, and to accept the whole Truth, and to know and

DIVINE SCIENCE STATEMENTS

enjoy freedom. Begin your work at once by saying, What has been done, I can do. I can realize myself to be whole. There is nothing in me, or of me that is not harmonious. Speak these words in faith and persist in acting in life with them; actions speak louder than words sometimes.

BE SINCERE IN YOUR EFFORTS

If you have sought in many ways and spent a fortune in your search for health, and have failed to find it, do not hesitate to try the Divine Science method, it will heal you. Your past experience has embraced methods of treatment based in the erroneous claim of physical causation, accompanied with hope of getting well, which at best, can only change one condition of belief for another. These changes have been brought about by going from one locality to another, change of scenery, or perhaps by a few little pellets; being made in belief only, and as to condition, these changes do not touch the plane of eternal Life, or Being; hence, do not touch our unchanging health. "God is the health of His people." The Christ of Divine Science method of healing proves that wholeness is to be enjoyed in Truth and nowhere else. It demonstrates that health is eternal; that success is ever at hand. Your past experience has been based in mere hope of getting well. Now, try the only true method of knowledge and faith-that of *being* well. "Be ye perfect, even as your Father in heaven is perfect." Perfect Being must necessarily precede perfect thinking; perfect thinking must precede perfect results either in words, deeds, or sensations. This is infallible law. Truth frees by proving that you are not bound.

If physicians have said that your case is incurable, if they have exhausted their skill upon you, and said there is no help for you, remember their skill consists in

CHRIST METHOD OF HEALING

administering external remedies and in performing operations. "In vain shalt thou use many medicines, for Thou shalt not be cured." Their skill is not that of bearing fruit of the Spirit of Truth, and creating anew, which is the only true demonstration of health there is. Healing is producing results direct from Spirit, or Principle. Give no place to what your friends have said about your case. Let your determination to succeed be a matter of wholly between God and you. God never pronounces against any one, and does not say that your case is incurable or hopeless. He has no method but the one perfection. He says: "Be whole, because I am whole." "Thy faith hath made thee whole." "Thou art loosed from infirmities." "My freedom is thine."

Age is not an obstacle in the way either knowing or demonstrating the freedom of Truth. Why limit the body by time, and the claim of age? It is eternal in idea and substance. The notion that mental faculties must fail with increasing years is a false one, and is as unreliable as is the belief that mental faculties, the brain, and entire body are the manifestations of Mind or Spirit, and Mind can never fail. Hence, you are always just old enough to be well, and to think right, and to know and remember all there is in Truth. Now, is just the right time to prove that you have health, are happy and satisfied. Now, is the time to bring eternal life and immortality to light, and bear witness of the truth of what you are.

Because you have spent large sums of money trying to get well, do not hold that as an objection against trying this method. When it is once settled in your consciousness that you want and can realize freedom and wholeness, the only question that should arise is: Do I want to realize it more than anything else; how much do I want health; what

DIVINE SCIENCE STATEMENTS

am I willing to do for it? Be not divided in your thought between money and what may be accomplished. Let neither money, time, nor anything, be as an obstacle in your way. Your determination will not falter if your purpose is one and undivided. Say, my birthright is health, wholeness and satisfaction, and think and act accordingly; do not barter it for any number of excuses. If necessary, give up all former habits of belief, speaking, and acting, and conform all to the Principle of Truth.

Jesus never denies that he is the Truth-the at-one-ment of God and man; but says, in the hour of seeming need: "To this end was I born, and for this cause came I into the world, that I should bear witness unto the truth." Each one should say: I am here to bear witness of the truth as much in the hour of seeming need as at any other time, and this is my time. To this end was I born. My existence bears witness of truth and life. I need no medicine. I cannot serve God and Mammon. The taking of medicine will not prove that I am eternal Life and Truth, or free from the liability of disease. I therefore declare that I am health and wholeness. I and my Father are one, and not two; hence, I am complete in Him, and find nothing in my existence to remedy. The I Am is sufficient unto all things needful.

As you have proved that all the claims made for external remedies are powerless to give the unchanging health and satisfaction for which you have sought, begin your work on the plane of Being, by being in God, and you will find what you have sought. If you have had no opportunity of studying Divine Science in a class, or have found no one to give you private instruction, who understands the Truth, then be as faithful to Truth contained in this little book as you have been in obeying the doctor's directions. Put yourself entirely in the hands of

CHRIST METHOD OF HEALING

Truth, and do as it directs. Argue not within yourself or with another about Divine Science.

Do not talk as if you were personally too good, or your opinions too true, to have brought about the diseased conditions from which you are seeking freedom, but that God was not too good to have brought them upon you, and that they must, therefore, be endured. Let the Christ knowledge speak in you in all things. Declare that *nothing I have believed in the past can prevent the true idea of God from being demonstrated in me.* Do not criticize this new and living method, Divine Science, nor condemn the statements made in this book; for surely, if you ask, and ask not amiss, it will be necessary that you assume, mentally, the attitude of one receiving. See, therefore, that you are willing to receive, by gladly acknowledging that you do possess what you have asked for. The truth herein recorded will be your teacher and healer, and will give you the necessary instruction to bring forth your conscious understanding of Truth.

Expect no one to devote their time to you without making some return for it. The law of giving is also the law of receiving; the entire business of the world is transacted through this law of exchange. Giving opens the channels for receiving. It is both spiritually and literally true from the individual standpoint that they who give, receive, and they who receive, give. Equal exchange, in the business world, is justice. The great desire, under general cultivation in the world, is that of getting, and giving as little as possible in return. This desire prevents many from realizing their divine opulence, for it is just the opposite of the Law of wholeness and success, which is, to render full measure for that which is given. There is no real freedom in this desire, nor is there any real possession in the desire to get

DIVINE SCIENCE STATEMENTS

something without rendering a just equivalent. As "the laborer is worthy of his hire," one might as justly demand another's money for nothing as to demand that one should give his time and labor for nothing. To render a just equivalent for all things, in our dealings with each other, is honorable, righteous and helpful. No teacher and healer ever thinks of charging for the Truth; hence, the charge is for the time spent in behalf of the students' and patients' welfare.

If healing is not instantly or quickly realized, be reasonable, sincere and willing to persevere. Do not say: I have given it a fair trial with a few treatments; but say to yourself: I am willing to believe that health is; hence, I am willing to say that I do not believe that I have any disease. Be as faithful in claiming that you have health, and that you are in a state of perfect harmony, as false belief has been in claiming to be diseased and inharmonious. Be as willing to persevere with Truth as you have been to take medicine and experiment with external remedies; and you will soon prove that Divine Science is all you need to bring out the full realization that God is your sufficiency. The instant your thought and belief is at-one with the idea of God, you will realize freedom. Do not postpone being well. Do not postpone for tomorrow what ought to be done today. The belief that you will receive by and by, keeps putting off, and prevents you from realizing in the sweet, happy now. You cannot speak the truth of Infinite Spirit without saying: I am well now; I am free now; I am health now; I am satisfied now; I succeed now. You cannot say: I hope for these things some time, and speak the word of God as He speaks it. Thus it is clear that the Christ Method is the demonstration of Principle. This is Life's "new and living way." Speak as God would speak, and your words will be living words, and your feelings, environments and success

CHRIST METHOD OF HEALING

will be shaped accordingly. Then you will be glad that you were told to say these things. The Infinite's idea is kept before you in this method. "Hold fast the form of sound words."

Avoid thinking, talking, or reading of sickness, or of any kind of trouble. Do not describe symptoms or sensations to any one. If friends or members of your own family ask after your feelings and symptoms, and you describe them, it prevents you from yielding thoroughly to the treatments; for when these conditions are talked about, they are still given form in memory; hence, they have not been given up. You can do much for yourself by avoiding everything that tends to keep in memory the condition from which you wish to be free. To prove the Christ Method, you are to be courageous, determined, and faithful, and think and act the truth that you have being in God now. Study Divine Science thoroughly, get an understanding of its law, and you will realize freedom and be able to liberate others from false claims and conditions. Do not attempt to mix or confuse Divine Science with former beliefs and opinions. As Good, or God, is no respecter of persons, say to yourself: I can do all that has been done. "He that believeth shall do the things that I do," is a promise to all. Yet, of myself, apart from the one All, I can do nothing. It is God in me who is doing the works. The law to be demonstrated is the Christ Method, and is mathematically exact. When wholeness is fully comprehended it is realized; and it is known that there is no disease in Truth. Ease, peace and eternal rest are in the truth at-one-ment. ONE IS THE NUMBER OF UNITY, not two.

PART TWO

§

INTRODUCTORY

INTRODUCTORY

§

To BE, is in the present. The act, is in the present.

The result of action is in the present. Action and the result of action have no power over Being, nor do they attempt to have. They are the power of Being expressing itself and expressed.

The true idea of a future and continuous Life is to be found in the eternity of the Life we now are. As the Life or Being that now *is*, is eternal, we are now what we shall ever be.

As eternity is a continuation of the present-a never ending now, and Being is eternal, to *Be* at all is to *Be* what *is* real and eternal now. Postponement of the use and full enjoyment of our divine inheritance is prophecy, but the fulfillment of all prophecy is in the present. Any and all action is in the present. It is not possible to begin the accomplishment of any work either in the past or future, hence, NOW is the beginning; so, "When ye pray, believe that ye receive, and ye shall have." There can be no result in the present without acting in the present, and no present action without Being. Now is the time to *Be*, to *Do*, and to have result or fruit of our doing. "Now is the accepted time." It is to be understood that Divine Science treatment when given to any one, no matter what the so-called disease is named, is to heal now. "To-day is the day of salvation." To-day is ever-present salvation.

This book is designed to correct the false race belief of separation of God and man; and the various theories of dualism arising therefrom. It is intended to eliminate the claim that man is ungodly, but can become godly through a process of doing and to establish him in the

DIRECTIONS FOR TREATMENT

consciousness that he is now altogether godly. False beliefs do not constitute man, nor have they anything to do with his existence; to realize his divinity and eternity it is necessary to refuse to entertain the false race beliefs about man.

DIRECTIONS FOR APPLICATION OF TREATMENT

God, the Good, being the Infinite Whole, the one All, it is God who is whole, and of whose wholeness is expressed in man. To ask in the name of God is to declare wholeness for ourselves; to acknowledge that it is already ours is true asking; God neither expresses nor knows any reality but wholeness, so to ask and ask not amiss is to believe ourselves whole, without spot or blemish. This is keeping the covenant of at-one-ment.

In the thoughts and words of God alone is to be enjoyed the full realization of wholeness. It is therefore intended that these treatments be used with the understanding that they are God's spoken word, the Truth of all living. We can only realize at-one-ment by being as God is, and thinking the same thoughts and speaking the same words. Do not hesitate to make statements for yourself, that are true of God-the Infinite Whole. In Truth there is nothing higher than wholeness and nothing lower. Realization of the truth of what you claim will be according to the faith you have in Truth. To believe that you are heirs of God, and to realize that you have received and are in possession of your inheritance, is to believe that you are every whit whole, and that every member and atom of your body is alive unto God now and ever will be.

To apply the following treatments, students should first to commit to memory the *Statement of Being* and

DIRECTIONS FOR TREATMENT

make it fully their own, then begin with treatment Number one and devote one day to its study and application. Read it over and over many times. The next day study and apply treatment Number two in the same manner; continue the same each succeeding day, with the treatment next in order, unto the end. Then begin over and rehearse in the same order. The *Statement of Being should* be read every day in connection with the treatment of the day. This practice will unfold to you the truth of Being and bring forth health, mental peace and successful effort. These lessons and treatments correct the erroneous belief of separation from God or Life, which is the underlying mistake made in attempting to solve life's problem from a false premise; and thus erase the false belief of a fall, and enable the student to understand and enjoy the truth that the problem of Life is already solved and demonstrated in his existence. Then is the truth of Principle seen to spring forth speedily in health, satisfaction, and success; which may be likened to a well of pure water springing up within you unto everlasting life.

Each statement of Truth, spoken with knowledge and Faith, believing that it is true, is sufficient in itself to heal. These treatments are all inclusive; they declare the Truth of God and man. As Truth heals, they are designed to heal every mental and bodily "disease." They are great freeing statements.

Before giving a treatment make the following statements: God is Infinite; and fully realize that it means God is All; and because the Good one is All, you are, and are what is; then know that all true claims are true of God, and what you claim that is true of God, you are, the same is the Son.

Go forth each day to perform your work or duties

DIRECTIONS FOR TREATMENT

clothed with the affirmations of Truth contained in the treatments, believing that you are whole, and are not subject to conditions, influences, or environments; you will find that by thus doing the will of God, the affirmations will prove to be a shield against all adverse beliefs and conditions; for, against Truth there is no law. "Thy righteousness is an everlasting righteousness, and Thy law is Truth." There is no power but of God."

THE ALL IS TRUTH
ERROR IS NOTHING

§

WHAT TO ACCEPT AND WHAT TO REJECT

§

STATEMENT OF BEING
THE BASIS FOR TEACHING AND DEMONSTRATING TRUTH
APPLICABLE IN ALL TREATMENT

I.

THERE can be put one All. This all in all is God and God manifested.

One is the number of unity.

Unity is forever the state or nature of One.

God being Infinite, there is no finite. He is all of Being, creative action and creation. "I and my Father are one."

God is Spirit, all of Life, Love, Truth, Substance, Soul and Intelligence, all of Knowledge, all of Power, all of Presence. Like expresses like; hence, man is Spirit, life, love, truth, substance, soul, intelligence, knowledge, power and presence, the exact image and likeness of God, co-eternal and co-equal with him.

Nothing can be manifested that is not, before it is manifested. As God alone *is*, it is *God* who is manifested in an ever-present creation.

That which is begotten of Spirit, is spirit. I am before I am manifested. Man is potential in God, and is expresser, co-worker and capable of doing His will, demonstrating the nature of Spirit.

BASIC STATEMENTS

Man Being and existence, created in the image of God's eternity and wholeness. There is one Spirit and one body. Individually, we are inseparable.

AT-ONE-MENT IS HARMONY

As God is the one all, all there is, is goodness.
"There is none good but One." The Truth for eternity is, "I am God and there is none else, * * * none like me;" hence, oneness is wholeness. The supposition that there is separation from God, that there is something that is not God, is false. It falls short of Truth, and in the scriptures is denominated sin, serpent, the adversary. The only seeming separation as adverse of God is false belief.

A good source cannot produce an evil result, nor can the method or act, by which the result is produced, be less perfect than the source; neither can the result be less perfect than the source and method by which it is produced.

HEALTH TREATMENT

AT-ONE-MENT IS SALVATION

"Of the Tree of the Knowledge of Good and Evil thou shalt not eat of it." The primary and spiritual meaning of eating, in the allegory, is identifying self with. To partake of anything means to assimilate and be one with that of which we partake. To believe that there is *something* that is separate from and is not God is to believe that there is something that is separate from and is not Good; to believe that there is anything that is separate from and that is not God, or Good, is to believe that there is an evil power capable of producing evil results. This, and all such beliefs are sensed as conditions which are looked upon as evil, the adverse alike of God and man. A supposition that creation is separated from God-something that is not-is no part of God or man, who though supposed to be twain are one Spirit. A false conception is no conception at all, and never comes to anything; out of nothing, nothing comes.

To ignore the Truth is to suspect that there is something that is not. Ignorance, therefore, is merely unsuspectingly taking things for what they are not.

"AGREE WITH THINE ADVERSARY QUICKLY"

A deviation from the Principle of at-one-ment-the unity of God and creation-is the only adversary of Truth.

That which *is*, is Truth. It is impossible for anything to *Be* and *be* Truth. It is a knowledge of Truth only that can agree with the adversary, by knowing that falsehood is false, and that a false supposition is nothing. It is a test of true consciousness to see the nothingness of nothing.

BASIC STATEMENTS

Non-resistance is the way of Life. "I am the Way." What I am is the way. I know that there is nothing the adverse of Truth. To agree that falsehood is false, is to agree with the adversary and let it be nothing. In Truth there is nothing to resist. To agree with the adversary quickly, it to agree that it is what it claims to be-the adverse of Truth. A false claim does not represent the Truth of anything that is. There is in Truth no sin or separation from God. There is no condemnation. "Neither do I condemn thee," is a test of knowledge and not of prejudice.

I.
TREATMENT

WHOLENESS

"God is the health of his people."

God is the One All; there is nothing to resist. God is Love; there is no one to fear, none to find fault with.

All that *is*, is Truth. All that I am is Truth. I am one perfect whole, harmonious throughout. I am the Spirit of health and harmony. All that I manifest is complete within me. My conception is immaculate. My faith (substance) reveals my wholeness. I enjoy life, freedom and happiness. My body is the perfect expression of the perfection I am. It has no Source of Origin but perfect Being. Every member is a member of righteousness and power. Every atom it comprises is Life. Every atom is eternal. All that *is*, is Spirit. "That which is born of Spirit is spirit." Now is my body spirit. In me all things are reconciled. There is no adverse belief, condition or disease, either in Me, my creative action or my creation. I am eternal Life, never failing health. I know that so-called sin, sickness and death, are not real. All erroneous beliefs are

HEALTH TREATMENT

forgiven, or given up. I know all that live are free from error. The gift of God is Eternal Life. Beside Truth there is no law.

II.

BASIC STATEMENT FOR TREATMENT
"KNOW THE TRUTH, AND THE TRUTH SHALL MAKE YOU FREE"

To know the Truth is to perceive and know what is, was and ever more shall be, the eternal. To be free in Truth is to *be* what *is* and is now free from error. What your highest conception of Divinity is, that claim to BE and you will press forward to the mark of your high calling in at-one-ment. "Put on the whole armor of God, that ye may be able to stand; "for Christ is the end of the law for righteousness to every one that believeth." The whole armor is the whole of God, God in his entirety.

II.

TREATMENT

PERPETUAL HEALTH, AGAINST INHERITANCE

"Make the tree good and the fruit good." I affirm these truths for myself; they are fully my own, they apply alike to all. I do this and demonstrate the Truth there is no mortal parenthood or inheritance, no mortal source or cause operating in creation at this time.

BASIC STATEMENTS

I an my Father are One.

I am infinite; Truth is my freedom. Therefore, there is no Finite.

Like produces like; Therefore, no production is unlike the Creator.

God is Spirit, the only Creator Therefore, there is no physical causation or Creation.

That created by Spirit is Spirit; Therefore, no created thing is of the earth and Earthly

We are conceived in Righteousness and born in True holiness; Therefore, we are not conceived in sin nor born in iniquity (inequality).

All forms are manifestations of Spirit; Therefore, there are no material forms.

We are immaculately conceived in the Spirit of Wholeness, and are begotten Of God; Therefore, we are not impurely conceived in separation nor begotten of the Flesh.

In the beginning God created Heaven and earth: Therefore, there is no material heaven or earth.

"Heaven and earth, the seas And all that in them is," are God expressed. God is always the God of the living; Therefore, there is no heaven, or earth, or seas, or anything therein, that is born of time or place, God is never the God of the dead.

HEALTH TREATMENT

The tree is good, and the fruit is good.
God is good, and I am good.
The Creator is good, and the creature is good.

God's will is done in creating earth as it is in creating heaven. There is no law over God. There is no law over man. The One all which I am is all law. Beside the word which is God, without which nothing is made, there is no Law.

III.

BASIC STATEMENT FOR TREATMENT

"I HAVE OVERCOME"

To overcome is to come over from the theory of become to Being, and know the Truth of the correct relation of Cause and effect existing between the Creator and creation. Being Source and Cause, is being that which includes all creation; this is dominion. It is true that I am hid with Christ in God; my possibility is the possibility of God idea; my existence is this possibility or idea made manifest; for beside God there is none other. It is God who says: "Be ye holy, because I am holy." As God's knowledge is omniscience there can be no knowledge that it is not.

Knowledge is free from suffering, failure, and dissatisfaction. For this reason, from the standpoint of at-one-ment alone can the false sense of them be erased. It is God, the *Infinite One*, who says, that to know self is to know all there is to know. We are neither fruitless nor deceived in claiming God-knowledge, absolute consciousness of truth; we are blessed of the Lord.

BASIC STATEMENTS

True knowledge is certain perception of the Truth of at-one-ment, the unity of God.

III.

TREATMENT

ADJUSTMENT
FOR HEALING OF ENVIRONMENT
"THE WORDS THAT I SPEAK, THEY ARE SPIRIT AND THEY ARE LIFE"

There is no enmity. I am infinite and all-pervading Love. I have manifested all things, and they live within me. I am both Love and loving in all that live and move and have being. I am unmoved by all that live. I move within and act upon all form. I am Love in the midst of all climates and changes of the weather. I am not affected by the wind, the storm, nor the calm. I am unchanged by either heat or cold. I, Love, possess and am master of all things. There is no power given in existing forms, conditions, circumstances, or events that I am not. All that I manifest is spirit and is life. I am perfect adjustment. My body is not subject to false sense of things; to disease, to mental conditions, or physical environment. There is no sin, mortality or corruption. My body is at one with the Source and Cause of all form. It is not the maker itself; neither is it the maker of other forms. It is subject to nothing. It exists within and is at-one- with all there is. I, who made it, and its life, intelligence, substance, and power. It is not sick, and there is nothing within its nature opposed to what these words imply.

HEALTH TREATMENT

IV.

TREATMENT

ILLUMINATION

DEHYPNOTIZES FROM ERRONEOUS BELIEFS OF SUBJECTION

God is not what he is through choice. Man is not what he is through choice. There is no optional nature to either God or man.

The allness of the all cannot choose between two or more different things what it will be. The I that I am beside whom there is none, has no choice as to the nature of Being. It is the nature of wholeness, Infinitude of Knowledge, Power and Presence to express itself. This is done within itself and unto itself.

Man is what he is just as God is what he is. As God is life, love, truth, substance, intelligence and power; so am I, life, love, truth, substance and power. Illumination is one. I am it; I am concentration; I am self-poised, self-centered and free. I am in no way subject to the law of cause and effect. I am it. There is no law over me, none to come against me. For there is none that I am not.

My senses are spiritual; I am their illumination. I observe all things truthfully. My house is now set in Order according to perfect illumination.

BASIC STATEMENTS

V.

BASIC STATEMENT FOR TREATMENT

THE WAY OF LIFE

"Whosoever hath not, from Him shall be taken even that Which he thinketh that he Hath.

"Take heed how ye hear: for whosoever hath, to him shall be given."

To claim to possess the opposite of what you are seeking, prevents the realization and enjoyment of what is sought.

To claim that you possess that which you have sought, brings the full realization and enjoyment of it.

Whosoever believes that he Is not whole, from him is taken away that which he thinks he has; the unfailing health of Being is not realized and enjoyed by believing that we are not whole.

Whosoever believes in his heart that he is whole, to him unfailing health and wholeness is realized and enjoyed here and now.

THE BROAD WAY
Error never claims life or Freedom for the present; it always hopes to become; hence, it does not testify of itself, nor bear witness of what the I am is.
Hereby, know we the claims of false belief.

THE NARROW WAY
Truth always claims to be Life Eternal and to be free now; hence, it testifies of all there is, and bears witness of what the I am is.
Hereby, know we the Spirit of Truth.

HEALTH TREATMENT

V.

TREATMENT

PERFECTION OF PURITY OF BODY

The Pure in Heart See God.

Therefore, I affirm in thought, word and act:

There is no death, error, or ignorance within me;	For "I am" Spirit, and Spirit is Life, Truth and Wisdom.
There is no hate, covetousness or pride within me;	I am Love, Justice and Perfection.
There is no doubt, fear or weakness within me;	I am Knowledge, Love and Faith.
There is no selfishness, prejudice or aversion within me;	I am all-pervading presence; I am no respecter of persons.
There is no sense of evil, disease or dissatisfaction within me;	I am Goodness, Ease, and Satisfaction.
I do not think evil thoughts;	I am pure in heart and clean in thought.
I know not failure;	For God is success.

"I and my Father are one, and not two."

BASIC STATEMENTS

I am free with the freedom of Truth. I am alive with God-life. I am at rest and at one with all that is. God, the All Life, is my life. In these affirmations I worship God in Spirit and in Truth. I am alive forevermore. I claim all that eternal life implies, and to *me it is given*.

VI.

BASIC STATEMENT FOR TREATMENT

"STRAIGHT IS THE GATE AND NARROW THE WAY WHICH

LEADETH UNTO LIFE; AND FEW THERE BE THAT FIND IT"

I have found the narrow way which leads unto life, it is Unity, I walk in the "New and living way." The few who find it are my Father and I, we see that the "Outer is as the inner"; the creature is as the Creator; that the tree is good and the fruit is good; and the All as one infinite Good. We see: "I and my Father as one." I, therefore, realize eternal Life and enjoy heaven here; for in at-one-ment God's will is done.

To believe that evil, sin, sickness and death are realities, and that we are subject to them, is to have other gods before Me. The desire naturally yields to what we believe has dominion over us. "Ye believe in God, believe also in me." "This is the work of God, that ye believe on Him whom God hath sent." Equality is the law that unites Father and Son, or Creator and creation.

HEALTH TREATMENT

VI.

TREATMENT

DOMINION OVER ALL SUFFERING

There is no evil power or thing.	All power is God, and all things are good.
There is nothing material.	All that is, is Spirit.
My body is not subject to pain or disease.	My body is Spirit, and is perfect peace and rest.
Feeling does not originate in the body.	Feeling inheres in thought.
I do not feel pain.	My thoughts are of God and are painless.
There is no sin in Mind.	There is but One Mind, and it is wholly Divine.
There is no sin in body.	My body is the expression of Mind.
There is no sickness in Truth.	Truth is perfect freedom.
There is no death in Life.	Life is All in All. I am Life.

BASIC STATEMENTS

VII.

TREATMENT

OPULENCE

"Let the word of God dwell in you richly." "I am that I am, and beside me there is none other." "I Am, is my name forever." I am perfect harmony. All my works are done in Truth; all My ways are just and right.

I am Opulence. I am Totality; the Universal and he abundance of the manifest universe.

I know no lack, want or poverty. I am the fullness of health, infinite supply and Omnipresent wealth. I am Omnipresence, Omnipotence and Omniscience, demonstrating my abundance continuously.

"All that is made, is mine."

HEALTH TREATMENT

VIII.

BASIC STATEMENT FOR TREATMENT

"HE THAT BELIEVETH ON ME, THE WORKS THAT I DO SHALL HE DO ALSO"

To believe on Jesus, the Christ, is to know that you are in the kingdom of God as his dear Son, and that you are just the same in being and existence as is Jesus, Christ. "And at that day ye shall know that I am in the Father, and ye in Me, and I in you." The Comforter that the Father sends, which shall abide with you, is the Spirit of Truth. *Now* is always the time to believe in the truth are, and be comforted.

VIII.

TREATMENT

TO DEMONSTRATE THE COMFORTER

NOW IS THE ACCEPTED TIME

I believe that Jesus Christ is come in the flesh, that the work of Christ is being done. 'The Law of the spirit of Life in Christ Jesus hath made me free from the Law of Sin and Death." I am the Light of the world, and can say:

BASIC STATEMENTS

There is no fear;	For God is all-pervading Love.
There is no fear of separation from God, within me;	For God is One inseparable Omnipresence.
There is no fear of sin, sickness, or sorrow within me;	For now am I saved, my health is established, and my joy complete
There is no fear of death, weakness, or want within me;	For God is my Life, strength and abundant supply.
There is no fear, anxious care or doubt within me;	For I dwell in Love, and Love dwells in me.
There is no fear that I shall become helpless and a burden to my friends;	For the gift of God is Eternal Life, I am life, ever restful, active, and free from Burden.
I do not fear age of body; there is no age;	For my body is eternal substance.
There can be no failure of mental faculties, sight or hearing;	For in God there is no failure. He is my unfailing sight and hearing.
God hath not given us the spirit of fear;	But of power, and of Love and a sound mind.

I fear not, doubt not, resist not. Love is without fear, I know not fear, I am Love. I am complete and perfect in God-love. I now realize that I am all for which I have sought. I am in the Holy of Holies, self-illumined. I demonstrate perfect health, peace and satisfaction.

HEALTH TREATMENT

I am at rest in my thoughts. I am clean in thought and pure in heart. I see God as All in All. I have no life or self-hood apart from God. I am satisfied and happy. I am God rest.

IX.

BASIC STATEMENT FOR TREATMENT

LIKE EXPRESSES LIKE

When an estate is bequeathed, there is a specified time for the heirs to possess it. Our inheritance is purity throughout; it is that in our mental and bodily existence we are spirit. Now is the time specified by the Eternal One for us to claim our Being, our sonship in God, "To-day is *the day* of salvation;" this inheritance is the redemption of our body.

IX.

TREATMENT

AGAINST BODILY LIMITATION AND FOR DEMONTRATION OF OPPORTUNITIES

"All power is given unto me in heaven and in earth."

The Holy Spirit is here and I am here.

BASIC STATEMENTS

Two things the reverse of each other cannot occupy the same place at the same time.

Because the Spirit is holy, I am holy.

Wholeness is my inheritance bequeathed by the inseparableness of the All. Now I am all possibility that I can ever be or express. I am *eternal* Life, and I manifest it fully. I am Spirit, and it is my day of perfect knowledge. I am baptized into Christ and have put on Christ. The one who anoints with the Spirit of Truth is God. I am perfect in thought, motive and feeling. I am harmonious in word, deed and sensation. I am accurate and definite in all I think and do. I am the idea of success. I am all opportunity, and know no limitation. I am sight, hearing, health, faith, power and understanding. I manifest all that I am. All my ways succeed. I am not a servant, but a son, radiating the light and glorifying the life of the Infinite One. My possibilities are immortal, incorruptible, unalterable. The whole earth and the fullness thereof is Mine. Thus is God glorified on earth. "All that the Father hath is mine." *Of all that Thou hast given me I can lose nothing.* Nothing that belongs unto Thee can be lost. This is inheritance or inherency. There is no corruption, no mortality, death is swallowed up of Life. There is no enemy. God is Life, and there is none beside.

"Be still and Know That I Am God."

HEALTH TREATMENT

X.

TREATMENT

SPECIFIC TREATMENT FOR DOMINION

Treatments-ten and eleven are to be used to heal of the desire for liquor and of the belief that man is under the dominion of appetite.

Speak the name of the one receiving treatment, and say-

I do not condemn thee. I love and am one with thee. Our Father we thank Thee for the knowledge that Thou art All, and art in all, as the ever-present Life and living good. As such, we worship Thee in the spirit of wholeness, and see Thy glory manifest in earth. In Thy truth we sanctify all things as Thou sanctifiest all with thy presence. Our brother acknowledges Truth. Enjoys thy presence and entertains Thee as his constant companion. He loves to affirm the Truth, that Thou hast made all things like unto Thyself, and hath placed no limitation upon them; Thou hast not measured thy spirit unto him. He partakes of thy inseparable and unlimited nature. Thy wholeness of Being is given unto him. He exercises absolute dominion and is subject neither to appetite nor desire. Dear brother, you cannot be tempted. There is no one to tempt and none to be tempted. You are whole, pure and good, there is nothing impure or unholy in you. You pronounce yourself good, you refuse to pronounce against God, you love to pronounce with Him, and declare your freedom.

BASIC STATEMENTS

XI.

TREATMENT

SCIENTIFIC TREATMENT
AGAINST DESIRE FOR LIQUOR

To God there is no idea or possibility of limitation; no *sensuous* appetite or desire; hence, dear brother, James, you are not limited, environed by, or subject to any seeming appetite or desire for liquor, or to the belief that you are. You cannot express anything real that does not represent Being; therefore, you are free in Truth at this time; nothing that binds or limits you.

Thou art, O God, pronouncing him good and very good, free and whole, for thou dost contain him at this time in Thy limitless Being and Love.

Dear Brother, listen to the voice of God speaking within you, saying, "You do not slumber in sense delusion; there is no sense delusion. You are no limited or controlled by desire. In truth you control desire. You have dominion over it. You do hear and understand My words of supreme freedom. You are free to witness My presence working in you. Listen, and understand what I say to you: liquor is neither the life, intelligence, substance, power nor peace for which you are seeking. It cannot give you strength, success, health, or satisfaction; nor can it prove to be a source and cause of happiness to you. You do not believe that you desire or need it; you know that it supplies no want; you know that you are immortal and are eternal life with Me. You are in no way dependent upon liquor for health, strength, success, or happiness. I, alone, am the source of all that you need. Your body is now radiant, strong, and

HEALTH TREATMENT

healthy with My presence. There is no darkness within you. You now understand that what I say to you is Truth. I am your Life, love, truth, substance and peace, and you are filled with perfect satisfaction at this time. *Behold! Thou art made whole."*

Amen!

XII.

TREATMENT

TRUTH FOR GENERAL BODILY HEALING

My life, substance, intelligence and power is God; there is nothing more, and nothing less. I am what I am, whole, perfect, without sin, or any disease, because God and God manifest is all there is.

I have not sinned; I do not fall short of Truth; I have not missed the mark of my high calling in Christ Jesus; I am not burdened with environments; I am not heavy laden with surrounding conditions; I am not weak with hope deferred; I am in my Father's kingdom, enjoying the power and glory of it; I am free, here and now.

BASIC STATEMENTS

XIII.

TREATMENT

FOR PERFECT SIGHT

I regard the holy presence of God within me sufficient for all demonstration of sight, health and prosperity. His presence within me is Omniscience, the All-seeing. I cannot see apart from Omniscience for I am not separated from its Omnipresence, and in It my sight has never failed; it is not dimmed; sight cannot fail; my eyes are the eyes of the all-seeing One; I see perfectly at this time. I have sought and found. No conditions of the past or of the present have any power to limit or environ me, no seeming condition can possibly reach or mar the sight that I am. I am ever and ever all-sufficient in God.

XIV.

TREATMENT

FOR HEALING OF ALL ACUTE DISEASE

Suggested from the allegoric Truth of the second chapter of Genesis, and used successfully by the author in pneumonia, chest troubles and different acute conditions.

A river of God flows out to water the garden now; from thence it becomes into Four heads. Your blood is the first head. This river flows perfectly in every organ and atom of your body. Your body is a river of God. Its rise and flow is God. It is the blood of God, the blood of life, the blood of love, of intelligence and power. It is the blood of Christ, free, unobstructed, strong, pure and healthy. The

HEALTH TREATMENT

obstructions that seem to be are not real. There is perfect circulation, and you are equalized from head to foot, free in every part.

The second head of this river of God is breathing. God now breathes the breath of life into you. Your breath has its rise and flow in God. There is no obstruction, no congestion. Your breath is the breath of God, of life, of love, of intelligence and power. It is the breath of Christ, unobstructed, strong, pure, healthy and free. You breathe freely, fully, deeply. Nothing binds or limits your breathing; its power is permanent and unlimited.

The third head of this river of God, whose rise and flow is God, is your perfect digestion and assimilation. God blends perfectly in you, and God-perfection is expressed perfectly in you now. You are One with God and One with your food, and are receiving, all that you do receive, perfectly, and are giving off, or forth, perfectly of what you have and are. There is a fourth head to this river of God, which is perfect generation. These all water every organ and atom of your body with the water of life. There is now direct generation from God in you; you are quickened anew from head to foot, and are perfect, whole, complete, healthy, full of the activity of Omnipotent power. You are a living son, radiating intelligence and health. These words of Truth are strength to your body, health to every part, sight to your eyes, and hearing to your ears.

BASIC STATEMENTS

XV.

TREATMENT

PERFECT DIGESTION

"All Thine are mine and All mine are Thine."

The Glorious liberty of my body is that of a child of God; which is heir of God and joint heir with Christ.

Digestion is Unity of Substance. Its source is God. The food I digest is one with Me. There is no conflict between Me and my food. There is perfect agreement and assimilation. Whether eating or drinking I do all to the glory of God. "I am the bread of Life." "I am the living bread which came down from heaven." The bread that I will give for the life of the world is my flesh. By eating my flesh and drinking my blood I identify them with myself, and express therein the life that I am.

By thus eating I dwell in Christ, and Christ dwells in me. This being perfect oneness, I am the Christ; so the law is now fulfilled that I live as the Father lives.

Explanation-Every one who applies this treatment sees that he lives as I live, and that we are entirely free from trying to digest food spiritually or literally supposed to be acquired from a source other than what we are, or what the I am is.

HEALTH TREATMENT

BRIEF SUMMARY

Being is God, is self-existing, the Fullness of the All. Being is not subject to power, life, or law. It is all power, life, and law. It is not subject to, dominated or environed by anything. The All in All knows nothing beside, nothing to dominate or environ.

Being is Inseparable; this proves man to be self-existing, eternal, forever and ever conscious of being in and of the inseparable whole. The inseparableness of the One Whole proves man to be higher than he has, or can ever be placed by human misbelief or mortal misconception. God-idea is with God, and is God, without which nothing is expressed that is expressed. It is the whole of man; it is "Spirit," which is both Soul and Body. It is life, substance, intelligence and power.

Divine Science reveals a higher, broader and deeper nature to man, and to all things, than any previous teaching except that of Christ. It is absolute freedom from the belief of the world's apostasy from God either by a fall or a supposition of becoming, a carnal or mortal mind, or a lower self.

There are no elements in matter, so called, of disease, lack or death, and no qualities but what are indestructible, hence eternal. This compels us to see that matter in its essential nature is free from disease, lack or death, and is therefore the direct expression of Spirit. This is the true standard consciousness which knows no corruption; in which "death is swallowed up of life;" in which the Universe is Spirit substance-One body; "we are all members of the body of Christ."

BASIC STATEMENTS

For sin, sickness, and death to be real or to be any part of man-the unit of Spirit, soul and body-they would have to be qualities of God or elements of indestructible matter; in either case they would be self-existing and eternal.

To see man as Spirit, at one with God, it is essential to see the nothingness of all false beliefs, the nothingness of nothing. To do this one should analyze them perfectly, as I were, and as he sees that no place can be found for them in the self-existing nature of Being, nor in the indestructible nature of the elements of matter, know that they must fade away into their native nothingness. There is no inharmony in expression; inharmony is human misbelief, the want of a knowledge of the perfect expression that is. Misbelief us out of harmony with knowledge. Truth makes free. It proves the One Whole to be free. How shall we dispose of matter in Divine Science? By seeing the truth of it. How shall we find freedom for our bodies? By knowing the truth of them. The Truth of anything is the freedom of it. If there were no truth in body, there would be no freedom of body. But instead there are Truth bodies and bodies free, and we have found them, so let it be.

www.ingramcontent.com/pod-product-compliance
Lightning Source LLC
Chambersburg PA
CBHW060852050426
42453CB00008B/953